Sacred Geometry Book of History, Meanings and How to Create Them

written by

Debbie Brewer

Book cover artwork by Orel Evgeniy

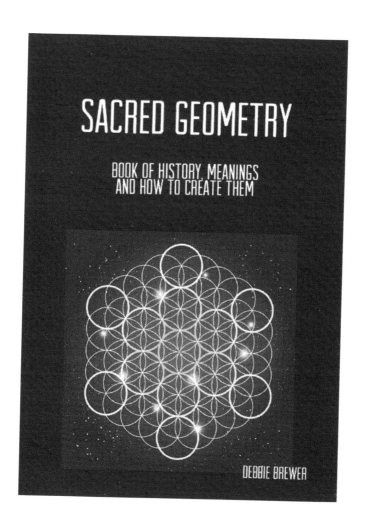

Also by Debbie Brewer

Poetry Treasures Series:

Volume One

Volume Two

Volume Three

Volume Four

Poetry Treasures: Special Edition

Driver Training Series:

What to Expect on your Driving Test

Step by Step Guide to the Driving Test Manoeuvres

Show me Tell me Questions for the Driving Test

Motorways; An Essential Guide to Driving on the Motorway.

Other Books:

Jack and the Friendly Aliens

Ethan and the Magic Hat

The Christmas Clock

Inspiration; Nuggets of Wisdom and Motivational Mantras

Easy Spells, Charms and Potions to Attract Money, Love and Happiness

The Spiritual Index, A Reference Book For All Things Spiritual

www.debbiebrewerauthor.com

Contents

Prologue

Acknowledgements

What is Sacred Geometry?

Simple Shapes and Numbers

Irrational Numbers

Fibonacci Numbers

The Golden Ratio

Golden Spiral

Significance of the Golden ratio

Three Dimensional Shapes

Platonic Solids

Using Simple Shapes and Numbers to Create Sacred Geometry

Flower of Life

Seed of Life

Fruit of Life

Egg of Life

Tree of Life

Metatron's Cube

Torus

Vesica Piscis

Reuleaux Triangle

Triquetra

Tetractys

The Symbol of Alchemy

Pentagram & Pentacle

Hexagram, Star of David & Solomon's Seal

Venus Cycle

Eight Pointed Star

Rose

Mandalas

Yantras

Sri Yantra

Conclusion

Glossary of Terms

References

Connect with the Author

Prologue

Dear reader,

Why is it that we are drawn to sacred geometry? What is it about these patterns that entice us? They start with simple mathematical shapes, that combine to create elaborate illustrations of such beauty and elegance that we marvel at them.

Beliefs, religious, spiritual and cultural, have been historically attached to them. The specific design and creation of each individual sacred geometric pattern is thought, among many cultures, not only to demonstrate an understanding of specific universal concepts, but to hold powers of mystical possibilities.

The aim of this book is to provide a brief basic understanding of the history, creation and meanings of sacred geometry for those who are new to the subject, and to open an insight into the beliefs placed upon them with the hope that it will inspire the reader's interest and imagination and urge them towards further research.

Enjoy learning how such simple shapes can evolve into inspiring and powerful patterns that weave through the fabric of our entire universe and reality.

Acknowledgements

With thanks to my mother for passing on her writing flair,

my father for his great spelling and grammar genes,

and my husband for his patience when I am in my writing zone

Dedicated to my children,

Ben and Samantha

Sacred Geometry
Book of History, Meanings
and How to Create Them

Debbie Brewer

What is Sacred Geometry?

Sacred geometry, in its simplest definition, is meanings ascribed to specific mathematical shapes and proportions.

Geometry is the study of spatial order using the measure and relationship of forms. (Lawlor, 1982).

The term, 'geometric' can be defined as patterns or shapes consisting of regular shapes or lines. The word 'geometry' comes from the Greek word, 'geos', meaning 'Earth', and 'metron', meaning 'to measure', leading to its literal translation of 'measuring of the earth' (Skinner, 2006). Its origins can be traced back to 3000 BC where the Egyptians and Mesopotamians used geometry to calculate lengths, areas and volumes.

Such shapes and proportions are found throughout the universe, in music, light, cosmology, and nature, in varying sizes, from miniscule particle examples, to enormous galactic dimensions.

Historically, for thousands of years, sacred geometry has been used in human art, architecture and meditation, becoming an integral part of many traditional cultures and involved at a deeper spiritual, philosophical and religious level.

Both the ancient Babylonians and Pythagoreans believed that numbers had symbolic meanings and were the building blocks to the universe. They recognised that geometric patterns were repeated throughout nature, such as the repeating hexagons in a honeycomb, or the recurring seed angle at the centre of a sunflower. Such patterns could, and still can, be found in humans, plants and minerals.

They believed that using numbers to design specific shapes and proportions, they could use the power of these creations to invoke deities, ward off evil, and bring forth prosperity.

Throughout history, examples of sacred geometric designs can be found in spiritual and religious places all over the world, including the ancient Far East, Egyptians, Indians, Greeks, Romans and Medieval Europeans.

In the fourth century BC, the Greek philosopher, Plato, put forward the belief that the Creator (or God), created the universe according to a geometric plan. He considered geometry to be the ideal philosophical language. (Lawlor, 1982). This idea underpins the principle of sacred geometry.

Indeed, eleven hundred years later, in the sixteenth century AD, the mathematician and astronomer, Galileo, said, "Mathematics is the alphabet with which

God has written the universe," and in 1611 AD, the philosopher Johannes Kepler stated that, "Geometry existed before creation. It is co-eternal with the mind of God... Geometry provided God with a model for the creation."

Hence, we can see how mathematical geometry and religious, spiritual and cultural belief have combined to become 'sacred' geometry.

Simple Shapes and Numbers

In the late sixth century BC, the Pythagoreans introduced geometric concepts to number symbols. They assigned the number one as a point, two as a line, and three as a triangle etc.

They considered odd numbers to be definite and masculine, and even numbers were indefinite and feminine. The exception, was the number one, which was considered both masculine and feminine, and the nature of unity.

These themes continued through Pagan, Gnostic and Christian theories, where terminology might have differed, but the meanings remained similar.

One - Monad

The number one, often called the Creator, First Cause, Divine One, Father, Unity, Permanence, the Foundation, and many more, is the most stable and the generator of all numbers. It symbolises singularity and leadership.

The Pythagoreans, (circa 600 BC), named it the monad, or noble number. It represents the 'whole'. For example, the universe is a monad as it is a whole, made up of the complete sum of many elements. Similarly, any individual planet is a monad, in that it is a whole sum of many elements. A monad can be any size and can be applied to anything that can be considered one unit, made up of the sum of its parts.

The monad is considered to be the origin of all thoughts in the universe and is the cause of truth, symbolising wisdom. It is the origin from which the universe emerges, it is the universe itself, and it is the centre to which everything will return., ie, point, seed and destination. (Lundy & Sutton et al., 2010).

It is associated with the sun as the centre of our solar system, and with chaos as the centre of the universe.

It is linked with the Greek god Apollo, god of music, poetry art, oracles, archery, sun, light medicine and knowledge, and the Greek Titan-god, Prometheus, god of fire.

The Point

Ancient mathematicians started with a dot and drew a circle around it. The first circle represents the number one.

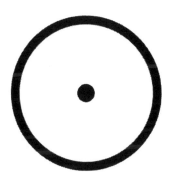

Point

This figure is also referred to as the 'First', 'Essence', 'Foundation' and 'Unity'.

The point has no dimension or space. It has no inside or outside. It is therefore the source for all that follows. (Lundy, 2008).

Some say this figure represents the sun. Others suggest, that as all measurements begin or end at a point, this figure represents the beginning and end of all types of creation.

Nicolaus Cusanus, the German theologian (1401-1464) said "God is an infinite circle whose centre is everywhere and whose circumference is nowhere."

Two - Duad

The number two represents natures dualities, such as hot and cold, male and female, separation and return, repel and attract, light and darkness, good and evil, love and hate, harmony and war, life and death. It is said to represent the dual masculine and feminine nature of God.

The duad is the origin of contrasts. It is the imperfect condition into which, according to the Pythagoreans, a being falls when he detaches himself from the Monad. (Pike, 1871).

It is considered to be balance and unity between opposing pairs and as the first feminine number, it is often referred to as the Mother.

It also represented contradiction, division, opposition, polarity, and reflection. It signifies ignorance, bringing balance to the monads wisdom, but can also symbolise a further wisdom, where ignorance gives birth to wisdom. (Malkowski, 2007).

The Pythagoreans named it the duad. While they held the monad in high respect, they despised the duad as its power created the underworld opposite the heavens.

As the first feminine number, it is linked with the Egyptian goddess Isis, goddess of fertility and motherhood.

The Line

As previously mentioned, the number two, or duad, represents reflection.

For 'one' to become 'many', the circle is transformed by a reflection, with each circle sharing the centre of the other. (Hobgood, nd).

The circle (one) must be reflected and a line will connect the two centres.

Line

The line is the first dimension. A separation from the point has created a direction. The stationary end is the point, or 'passive'. The other end is 'active' as it can move and rotate. (Lundy, 2008).

Greek philosophers called the duad 'audacity', because of its boldness in separating itself from the Divine One. Hence, it also symbolises the anguish of separation and tension in the desire to return to oneness.

Three - Triad

Three is considered to be the number of harmony between body, mind and spirit, or balance, strength and stability, or past, present and future, or beginning, middle and end.

As the monad is not considered a number, rather, it is unity, the number three is therefore the first odd number, and is male.

The Pythagoreans called this the triad and It was the first number to make actual the potentialities of the monad, the first to make a shape or plane. It signified the beginning, the middle, and end; childhood, adulthood, and maturity; birth, death, and re-birth. (Emerson, 1996).

It is also said to represent friendship, peace, justice, prudence, piety, temperance, and virtue and is associated with the three primary colours; red, yellow and blue.

It holds wisdom as it represents knowledge, and is sacred as it is derived from the sum of the monad and the duad, (the Father and the Mother) ie, 1 + 2 = 3.

It is linked with the Roman god, Saturn, the ruler of time.

The Triangle

The triangle contains three points and three lines. It represents balance, stability and strength.

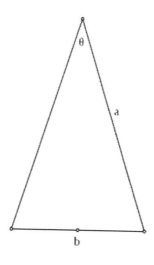

Golden Triangle

In sacred geometry, a 'golden triangle', sometimes called the 'sublime triangle', can be created by bisecting a 'golden rectangle' (see page 61), from one corner to its opposite corner, thus creating a triangle where its three sides and angles have a 2:2:1 proportion.

This means the two long sides are the same length, and the shorter length is exactly half. Similarly, the most acute angle is half the size of the two equal larger angles.

The sum of the angles of a triangle is 180°, so the base angles are 72° each and the acute angle is 36°.

Golden triangles can be used to make golden pentagrams. (See page 115).

Equilateral triangles are also used in sacred geometry.

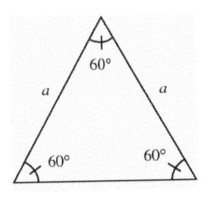

Equilateral Triangle

These have equal lengths and all internal angles are 60°. This shape is noted in the Vesica Pisces, (see page 100), the Reuleaux triangle, (see page 105), and the Triquetra, (see page 108).

The Pythagoreans believed the triangle symbolised light, health and wisdom. The ancient Egyptians thought it was a symbol of beautiful fertile land. In Hinduism, a point down triangle represents Shakti (female energy), and upward pointed represents Shiva (male energy). In ancient Europe, a point down triangle meant water flowing downward, and a point up triangle meant male fire and flames. (Tana, 2009).

Four - Tetrad

The Pythagoreans called the number four, the tetrad and it was considered to be the root of all things.

Pythagoras said that a man's soul was a tetrad, which consisted of the powers of the mind, science, opinion and sense.

It represents impetuosity, strength, and virility, and the secondary colours; green, orange, purple and cyan.

It is considered to be the key keeper of nature, as it is associated with four of the elements; earth, air, water and fire.

Tetrad is associated with justice, wholeness and completion. There are four seasons, four ages of man, and four directions (north, south, east, west). (Hobgood, nd).

The tetrad is linked with the Roman God, Hercules.

The Square

A square has four equal sides and four equal angles. In sacred geometry, the importance of the square, is its diagonal.

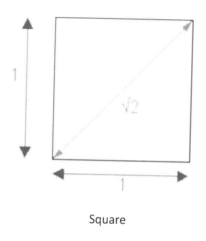

Square

If each side of the square is 1 unit in length, then the length of the diagonal is the square root of 2, which is an irrational number (see page 55).

The square symbolises the imposition of structure upon the earth. It has fixed straight rigid lines providing strong and steady foundations. It represents balance, community and integrity and is considered to be a stable shape, suggesting honesty, rationality, order, peace, solidity and equality. (Dimurlo, 2013).

The Square and the Circle – 'Squaring the Circle'

Combining the square and the circle represents the fusion of heaven and earth.

'Squaring the circle' means producing a circle overlaying a square, so that either the circumference of the circle equals the perimeter of the square, or the area of the circle equals the area of the square.

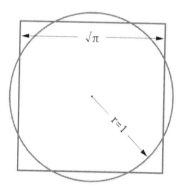

Squaring the Circle

The squaring of the circle represents an attempt to unite two opposites, which cannot be united, such as body and soul, earth and sky, or spirit and matter. "The circle in the square could represent the human being who was seen as an earthly vessel containing a divine essence." (Lieben, 2018).

According to the ancient Greek philosopher, Empedocles, circles represent the spiritual because they are infinite with no end. The square symbolises the material because of the number of physical things that come in fours, such as four seasons, four directions and four elements, earth, air, fire and water. (Beyer, 2019).

The squared circle is considered to be a perfect form and was used in the design of many religious buildings.

Most mosques are constructed around the symbolism of the squared circle in order to conduct energy in a particular manner.

Hagia Sophia

Above: The Hagia Sophia in Turkey, built in 532 AD, is one of the oldest surviving religious buildings in history which used squared circle geometry in its design.

Five - Pentad

The Pythagoreans called the number five, the pentad and it holds several meanings.

It represents a hand, and also marriage, as it is a union of male and female numbers, ie, $2 + 3 = 5$.

Importantly, it symbolises the fifth element, ether, which Pythagoras said permeated the four other elements of earth, air, fire and water, as the basis of life.

The pentad can be referred to as 'equilibrium' as it divides the perfect number 10 into two equal parts.

It represents all superior and inferior beings and is associated with mystic development, reconciliation, alternation, immortality and sound.

Spiritually, the number five is the number of manifestation, as it links all the five elements which contain all the components for creation. It aligns to freedom, joy and bliss and represents faith in action and mindful connection to nature. (Love, 2019).

The pentad was linked with the Roman god, Mercury, the messenger of Jupiter.

The Pentagon

As the pentad is a union of male and female, ie, 2 + 3 = 5, the pentagon shape represents life and regeneration. It can be formed by drawing a line from the centre of the circle to its outer edge, and then four further similar lines, each being 72° from the previous one. Then join the outer points on the edge of the circle with a straight line.

Pentagon

Every angle inside the pentagon is 108°. This number is sacred in Hinduism, Buddhism and Jainism. The average distance of the Sun and the Moon to the Earth is 108 times their respective diameters which has ritual significance in many cultures. There are 108 'pithas' (sacred sites in India). In yoga tradition, there are 108 'upanishads' and 108 'marma' points (sacred places of the body). (Rea, 2007).

From the pentagon, a sacred golden pentagram can be made using golden triangles. (See page 115).

Six - Hexad

Six is referred to as the hexad.

It is an important number because it is thought to be a balanced number and contains the elements of immortality. It is omnisufficient because it is made up of sufficient parts for totality, ie, 3 + 2 + 1 = 6.

It was therefore called the 'perfection of all the parts', and represents the creation of the world.

The Pythagoreans recognised this as the first perfect number, where all the number divisions, excluding itself, when added together, equal the number itself, ie, 3 + 2 + 1 = 6. This was held in high esteem as perfect numbers are rare. The ancient Greeks recognised just four perfect numbers: 6, 28, 496, 8,128. (Yogev, 2018).

As well as the pentad, the hexad was also a symbol of marriage, because it's shape, the hexagon, is formed by the union of two triangles, believed to be male and female.

It was considered to be sacred to the Greek god, Orpheus the musician, as the Greeks believed that harmony and soul were similar in nature and that all souls were harmonic.

"Six is a number perfect in itself, not because God created all things in six days; rather, the convert is true God created all things in six days because the number is perfect." – Saint Augustine, The City of God.

The Hexagon

The hexagon is a regular six sided shape. Each internal angle is 120°. It can be made by dissecting a circle through its centre three times, creating six equal slices each with an acute angle of 60°. The outside edge of each slice can then be joined by a straight line to make the hexagon.

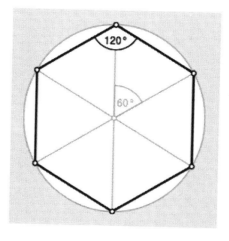

Hexagon

The hexagon can be considered one of the most powerful and fascinating shapes. It is one of the principal governing patterns that is dominant in the natural world, such as in the honey combe of honey bees, as they are the most efficient way to fill a space with the least amount of material. They are even found in the core of the double helix macromolecule forming the structure of human DNA. (Oldale, 2017).

From the hexagon can be made the Star of David and the Seal of Solomon. (See page 119).

Seven - Heptad

Seven is referred to as the heptad and is sacred in many cultures.

The Elohim of the Jews were the seven archangels controlling the planets. In ancient Mesopotamia, the creation story was referred to as the Seven Tablets of Creation.

According to Jewish and Christian old testament, the world was created in seven days, Noah's dove returned seven days after the Flood, and there are seven deadly sins.

The ancient Egyptians mapped seven paths to heaven.

The new born Buddha took seven strides.

Allah created a seven layered Islamic heaven and Earth.

The ancient Babylonians believed there were seven steps to the ascent to heaven. They divided the phases of the moon into four parts, each divided into seven days, and though not accurate, this gave us our defined week as a measure of time and from this, many cultural and religious rituals were based around the number seven elevating it to a magical number.

In Yogic belief, there are seven chakras in our bodies, the seventh symbolising the joining of male and female energies in balanced union and the fusion of the lower self with the higher self; the attainment of unified consciousness and spiritual awakening. (Scott, 2019).

The Heptagon

The heptagon (sometimes called the septagon) is a regular seven sided shape formed by dividing a circle into seven identical slices and joining their outer edges with a straight line.

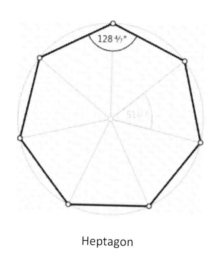

Heptagon

Seven is also representative of the head, whereby there are seven windows; 2 nostrils, 2 eyes, 2 ears, and a mouth.

The heptagon is special as, unlike the other regular polygons, it is the only regular geometric shape whose angles cannot bisect a circle to a whole number.

Therefore, it is symbolic of the unknowable, the seeking of wisdom, and sound. (Silva, nd).

The Heptagon also represents the Holy, or Great Spirit, embodying God's manifesting power. It is considered to be a force of creation from which all life flows. (Champoux & Buehler, 1999).

Eight - Ogdaad

The sacred number eight was referred to as the ogdaad. It was the number of the first cube, with eight corners, and was considered to be an 'evenly even' number, as eight can be divided into two fours, and each four can be divided into two twos, and each two can be divided into two ones, ie, the monad.

The ancient Greeks called the ogdaad the 'little holy number'.

In Christianity, eight is the number of resurrection and the number of people saved on Noah's ark. It was on the seventh day that Jesus was raised, the Sabbath, making Jesus' resurrection on the eighth day, Sunday, which was considered to be the first day of the week and the day of the New Creation. Hence, Christian churches built in the Byzantine period, were eight sided structures. (Hunt, 2007).

Eight is associated with beginnings, resurrection, salvation and super abundance. (Beyer, 2019).

The ancient Babylonians believed there were seven spheres and an eighth realm, the fixed stars, where the gods lived. Hence they associated the number 8 with paradise. In Buddhism, eight is considered lucky because of the eight petals of the lotus flower, a plant considered lucky and a favoured Buddhist symbol. (Stewart, 2005).

The Octagon

The octagon is a regular eight sided shape, formed by dissecting a circle through its centre four times, creating eight similar slices, each with an acute angle of 45°. The outside edge of each slice can then be joined with a straight line to make the octagon.

Octagon

The internal angles of the octagon are all 135°.

In Christianity, the octagon symbolises regeneration and rebirth. The font is usually octagonal as a place of regeneration. (Ashley, 2014).

Octagons figured highly in the Renaissance period. Buildings constructed during this time made use of the octagon shape as it was considered to be one of the best geometric solutions for centrally designed ecclesiastical architecture. Architectural drawings by Leonardo da Vinci frequently displays his use of octagons, more so than any other shape. (Reynolds, 2010).

Octagons can be formed by overlapping squares. They emphasize duality, such as male and female, or spiritual and material, or positive and negative. The octagon balances them. (Beyer, 2019).

Nine - Ennead

The Pythagoreans called the number nine the ennead. It is sacred because it is the first square of an odd number, ie, 3 x 3 = 9.

The number nine is the largest digit. As it falls short of the perfect number ten by one, it is associated with failure.

As ten is considered to be infinite, the ennead is the limitless number. Conversely, it is also linked with boundary and limitation because it gathers all numbers within itself. It surrounds the other numbers as the air surrounds the Earth, leading it to also be called the 'sphere of air'.

The ennead was often thought to be evil because it was an inverted six.

In Hinduism, there are nine universal elements; earth, sky, water, air, fire, space, time, soul and mind. There are also nine rasas (emotions); love, joy, wonder, peace, anger, courage, sadness, fear and disguise. Furthermore, they believe that life is made of nine elements: the three Gunas,(ingredients); sattva, rajas and tamas, the three functions; creation, preservation and destruction, and the three factors; time, space and causation. (Kumar, 2017).

Ancient Egyptians had nine gods and goddesses. Collectively, they were known as the Great Ennead. They were Ra, his children Tefnut and Shu (water and air), and their children Nut and Geb (sky and earth), and their children, Isis, Oisiris, Set and Nephthys. (Rogers, 2010).

The Nonagon

The nonagon is a regular nine sided shape formed by dividing a circle into nine identical slices, each with an acute angle of 40°, and joining their outer edges with a straight line.

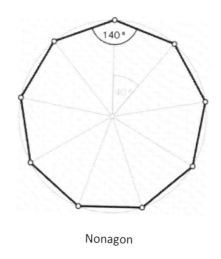

Nonagon

All internal angles of the nonagon are 140°.

The Hebrews called the nonagon a symbol of Immutable Truth.

When all the edges of a nonagon are connected, we construct shape called an Enneazetton.

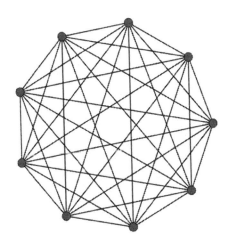

Enneazetton

This figure is referenced in modern day science. Although it is hard to visualise, this is an eight dimensional shape, having facets extending into seven further dimensions. (Rogers, 2010).

Ten - Decad

Ten was referred to by the Greeks as the decad. It was considered to be the greatest of all numbers, and as such, the 'perfect number'.

Pythagoras said that ten is the very nature of number, because when you arrive at the decad, you return to unity, or the monad. It symbolized both heaven and world. (Hobgood, nd)

It also symbolised the unwearied, because, like God, it was tireless.

The Pythagoreans associated the decad with the Greek god, Atlas, who carried the numbers on his shoulders.

They considered the number to be similar to the monad, but held it up to be a unity of a higher order. (Godwin, 2004).

The Decagon

The decagon is a regular ten sided shape, formed by dissecting a circle through its centre five times, creating ten similar slices, each with an acute angle of 36°. The outside edge of each slice can then be joined with a straight line to make the decagon.

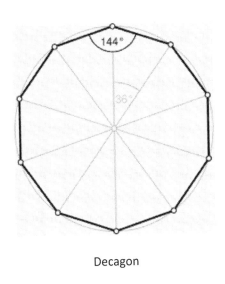

Decagon

All internal angles of the decagon are 144°.

As it tends towards a circle, the decagon represents a degree of attainment and wholeness achieved during a journey in preparation for transcendence into another field of consciousness. It symbolises the wholeness of the source, or unity, or monad, from which the self is originated and is contained. (Garant, 2011).

Irrational Numbers

There are many different types of numbers.

For example, a rational number can be written as a ratio or fraction:

1.5 can be written as 3/2

7 can be written at 7/1

Irrational numbers are those which cannot be expressed in a fractional form.

A common example of this is π, also written as Pi.

Pi cannot be written down as a fraction.

Another defining factor of an irrational number is that it does not terminate or repeat. Their decimal goes on unending.

For example: π = 3.141592653589793238462..... and does not stop.

Pi is important to sacred geometry because it is the ratio of a circle's circumference to its diameter. Pi is also a constant number, meaning that for all circles of any size, Pi will be the same.

According to some Hebrew traditions, Pi is symbolic with the Creator's infiniteness, and infinity in time, space, love, peace, harmony, omniscience and more. "Did God purposely hint to the profundity of creation in this simple yet fascinating ratio that he knew we would come upon? Contained infinity. That's a description of Pi, and a description of the creation itself." (Welman, 2016).

Fibonacci Numbers

The Fibonacci sequence was first recognised by the Indian mathematician, Pingala, circa 250 BC.

It became known as the Fibonacci sequence when Italian mathematician, Leonardo of Pisano, who was known as Fibonacci described the derivation of the sequence of numbers using the analogy of an idealised rabbit population.

In the Fibonacci sequence, we start with the number 1.

To this, we add the second number 1.

This gives the third number 2.

We then add the second and third numbers together (1 + 2) which gives us the fourth number, 3.

We then add the third and fourth numbers together (2 + 3) which gives us the fifth number, 5.

We then add the fourth and fifth numbers together (3 + 5) which gives us the sixth number 8

And so the pattern continues ever on. The next number in the sequence is always found by adding up the two numbers before it.

This gives us the Fibonacci numbers:

1, 1, 2, 3, 5, 8, 13, 21, 34, 55, 89, 144, 233, 377, 610, …..

Interestingly, no even number is ever next to another even number in the series.

Also, after the first sixty numbers, the last number starts to repeat.

Even more interesting, is that the 216th number in the Fibonacci sequence is 6192204516665901352286753878632978742693961 2 and if you add up all these individual numbers, they add up to 216.

This specific number is significant among spiritualists, as it is believed that the hidden name of God contains 216 characters.

Also, 6 x 6 x 6 = 216 which represents the Divine Trinity.

The number 216 is referred to as Plato's number, because the Greek philosopher Plato (circa 400 BC) recognised the fact that 6 x 6 x 6 = 216, where 6 is one of the numbers representing marriage as a product of the female number two, and the male number 3. (Kahn, 2013).

However, the number 216 itself, is not a Fibonacci number.

Fibonacci numbers are very apparent in nature. For example, in trees, the main trunk grows until it produces a branch, which creates two growth points. One of the new stems branches into two, while the other stays dormant. This branching pattern is repeated for each new stem, thus displaying the Fibonacci sequence.

Humans have two hands. Each one has five fingers. Each finger has three parts and are separated by two knuckles. All of these figures fit into the Fibonacci sequence. Or is this a coincidence? (Simmons, nd).

The Golden Ratio

The golden ratio, also often referred to as the 'golden number', 'golden section', 'golden mean', and 'divine proportion', is also an irrational number, called Phi. The value of Phi is 1.618033988749895…. and so on. Remember, as an irrational number, it does not terminate or repeat.

But how do you find the golden ratio?

Phi can be derived from the Fibonacci sequence. If you take a number from the sequence and divide it by the number before it, you get a series of numbers that tend towards Phi as shown below:

1 / 1 = 1   2 / 1 = 2

3 / 2 = 1.5   5 / 3 = 1.666

8 / 5 = 1.6   13 / 8 = 1.625

21 / 13 = 1.61538461

and the sequence continues, getting closer and closer towards the value of Phi.

You can further visualise the golden ratio using the following diagram:

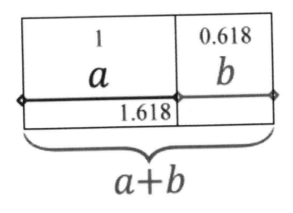

Golden rectangle

This rectangle is called the 'golden rectangle'.

From the dimensions of the golden rectangle, we can see that the longer length, a + b is to a, as the shorter length, a, is to the even shorter length b.

Or, you could say, the ratio (a + b) : a, is the same as the ratio a : b.

In words, the ratio of the larger length (a) to the smaller length (b) is exactly the same as the ratio of the whole length (a + b) to the larger length (a).

To mathematically calculate Phi, the value is 1 + √5/2, or one plus the square root of five over two.

Symbolically, the golden ratio links each new generation to its ancestors, preserving the continuity of relationship as the means for retracing its lineage. (Rawles, 2012).

The Egyptians thought the golden ratio was sacred, and hence called it the 'sacred ratio'. It was highly regarded within their religion. They incorporated the golden ratio in the arrangement of their temples and evidence of it can be found in the pyramids. (Holloway, 2013).

Golden Spiral

The golden spiral, (or Fibonacci spiral as it is also known), is important to sacred geometry because its logarithmic growth factor is the golden ratio. This means that the golden spiral gets wider (or further from its starting point) by a factor of Phi for every quarter turn it makes.

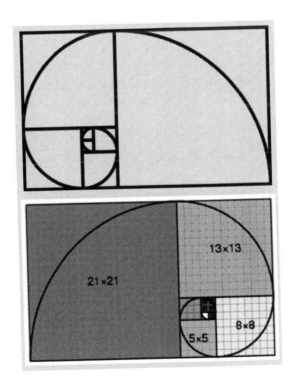

Golden Spiral

In Celtic symbology the golden spiral was used to decorate numerous artifacts, as a way to step outside the physical plane and enter a gossamer domain where dreams and intuition take hold of awareness.

The spiral spiritually represents the path leading from outer consciousness (ie. materialism, external awareness, ego and outward perception), to the inner soul (enlightenment, nirvana and cosmic awareness). The spiralling rings mark the evolution of humankind. (Venefica, 2013).

"The human mind always makes progress, but it is progress made in spirals." – Madame de Stael, circa 1800 AD.

Significance of the Golden Ratio

The golden ratio is extremely significant in sacred geometry.

The Golden Ratio in Nature

In the natural world, there are numerous examples of the golden ratio.

In plants, the seed heads at the centre of a flower grow in a spiral and the amount of turn of each seed head to create the spiral is a ratio of Phi to the previous seed. This gives the seeds the best possible exposure to rainfall.

Golden spirals can be seen in snail shells and seashells, goats horns and spiders webs. They can also be seen in spiral galaxies and satellite images of hurricanes and many more instances.

In dolphins, the eyes, fins and tail all fall at golden ratios to the dolphins body.

The leg and body ratios of an ant are defined by the golden ratios of its length.

In fact, the list of examples is enormous and impossible to fully list here.

The golden ratio is also evident in many human features.

In the human face, the mouth and nose are each positioned at golden ratios of the distance between the eyes and the bottom of the chin.

The length to the width of the of the face is a golden ratio.

The distance between the lips and where the eyebrows meet to the length of the nose is a golden ratio.

The length of the mouth to the width of the nose is a golden ratio.

The width of the nose to the distance between the nostrils is a golden ratio.

The distance between the pupils to the distance between the eyebrows is a golden ratio.

While you can argue that we are not all identical, and therefore the golden ratio is not exactly apparent, when you average the values across a large population, the values tend towards Phi. Some say that the closer a person's facial proportions match the golden ratio, the more attractive they appear to be. (Meisner, 2012).

Similar proportions can also be found in many other parts of the human body.

The Golden Ratio in Architecture

The ancient Egyptians generally believed that the presence of the golden ratio in architectural design provided a sense of balance and equilibrium as well as being pleasing to the eye. (Holloway, 2013).

There are many ancient constructions that exhibit the golden ratio. For example, Stone Henge, built in 3100 BC in England, has golden ratio proportions between its concentric circles.

The Parthenon in Athens, a Greek temple for the goddess Athena, built in 468 BC, also displays several dimensions in line with the golden ratio, including its height to its width.

The Castle of Chichen Itza, built by the Mayans in the eleventh century AD, is a temple to the feathered serpent god Kukulcun, and has golden ratio proportions with the interior walls placed so the outer spaces are related to the central chamber by the golden ratio.

Similarly, golden ratios can be observed in the architecture of The Great Mosque of Kairouan, Notre Dame in France, The Taj Mahal in India, The Eiffel Tower in France, The CN Tower in Toronto... and the list goes on.

The Golden Ratio in Art

As with architecture, there are many examples of the use of the golden ratio in art.

Leonardo da Vinci was known to have made good use of this ratio. In his famous painting, The 'Mona Lisa', completed in 1503 AD, he appears to have used the golden ratio in the construction of her face.

Mona Lisa

During the Renaissance, the golden ratio was called the Divine Proportion and it most commonly appeared in religious paintings. In Leonardo da Vinci's painting of 'The Last Supper', completed in 1498 AD, the golden ratio is extensively used in all the key dimensions of the room.

The Last Supper

Many more examples of the use of the golden ratio in art can be found, famously in Raphael's 'The School of Athens', Michelangelo's Sistine Chapel ceiling, Botticelli's 'Birth of Venus', and more.

Some modern art books suggest that it is better to position objects to one side of a painting, rather than central to it, as such a design is more pleasing to the eye. Hence, artists will often use the golden ratio to select the placement of objects within their artwork.

Even famous sculptures have been known to exhibit golden ratio proportions, such as the Venus de Milo sculpture of the goddess Aphrodite, created in 130 BC

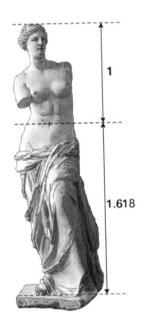

Venus de Milo

Three Dimensional Shapes

As well as being possible in any size two dimensionally, sacred geometry is also significant in three dimensions.

The Sphere

Sphere

The sphere represents the ultimate expression of unity, completeness, inclusion and integrity. In a sphere, all measurements are equal, regardless of its size. Everything can be created from the sphere. It is a container that can hold all of the other forms, and is considered to be the essence of the divine feminine and the motherly womb of spirit. (Krystleyez, 2018).

The Pyramid

A pyramid is supposed to have the power of preservation. The Egyptians developed the geometry to build them with extreme accuracy for their Nobles to lie in after death in order to preserve them. It is also considered to be able to channel energy.

Pyramids

The base of each pyramid is a square, and its perimeter is equal to the circumference of a circle, whose radius is equal to the height of the pyramid. Therefore, the ancient Egyptians were in fact, squaring the circle.

"The architects of the Great Pyramid of Giza were extremely wise beings, with an advanced knowledge of math and astronomy far beyond the standard of their time." (Solà-Soler, 2012).

Platonic Solids

The Platonic Solids were named after the Greek philosopher, Plato, (429-347 BC), who wrote about them in his treatise, Timaeus. (Usvat, nd). They are considered to be the five perfect shapes derived from dividing a sphere into three-dimensional forms.

The five Platonic solids are; the tetrahedron, the hexahedron, the octahedron, the dodecahedron, and the icosahedron.

They act as a template from which all life springs, and as such, are the building blocks of life. They are said to relate to the five elements; fire, earth, air, water and ether, and the five senses; sight, smell, taste, hearing, touch. Combining the five senses with the five elements creates the vehicle or body necessary to experience three dimensional space and time. The Platonic solids are seemingly perfect templates in the quest for balance and harmony within the constraints of three dimensional space and time. (Garant, 2012).

To be considered a Platonic solid, the three dimensional shape has to fulfil the requirement of equality by repeating identical corner angles, edge lengths, and surface shapes around the sphere.

They must conform to the following rules:

Each formation must have the same shape on every side.

The octahedron, tetrahedron and icosahedron must have equilateral triangle faces.

The hexahedron must have square faces.

The dodecahedron must have pentagonal faces.

Every line on each of the formations must be exactly the same length.

Every internal angle on each of the formations must be the same.

Each shape must fit perfectly inside a sphere, with all the points touching the edges of the sphere with no overlaps.

The Tetrahedron

A basic tetrahedron can be visualised as a pyramid, but with a triangular base, with every triangle being equilateral. Using the symbol for the Fruit of Life (see page 90), this can be built into the 'Star Tetrahedron'.

The Star Tetrahedron

Plato considered the tetrahedron to represent the element fire. In modern times, it is associated with creativity and inspiration.

It is said to connect heaven and earth as one, the spiritual world aligning with the earth plane. (Ashley, 2014).

The Hexahedron

The hexahedron is a cube, which can be formed using the symbol for the Fruit of Life (see page 90).

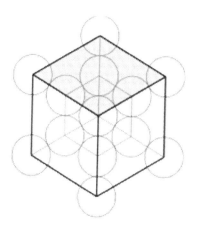

Plato considered the hexahedron to represent the element of earth, but the cube has many more religious and cultural significances.

In the Book of Revelation, heavenly Jerusalem is described as a cube. Also, the 'Oracle' in Solomon's Temple is a cube.

In medieval times, the Christian cross was an unfolded cube, and many cathedrals were built on a footprint of this design.

The Kaaba is a cube shaped building at the centre of Al-Masjid Al-Haram (The Sacred Mosque) in Mecca and is the most sacred site in Islam.

The cube is the symbol of stability, permanence and geometric perfection, and can be visualised as the truth.

It is the counterpart of the sphere, and some say, in essence, it is the squaring of the circle. (Jaffe, 2001).

In modern times, the cube is representative of the base chakra and the foundations of the earth to the foundation of the heavens.

The Octahedron

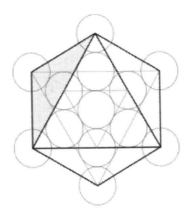

Plato considered the octahedron to represent the element of air. In modern times, it is associated with the heart chakra and the communication of compassion.

This represents reflection, compassion, healing, forgiving and acceptance. In spirituality, this shape is used in meditation to help understand the true nature of the self. (Patinkas, 2014).

The Dodecahedron

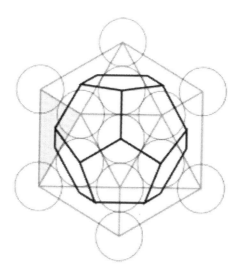

As the dodecahedron had twelve faces, Plato linked this to the twelve constellations of the zodiac and considered it to be the symbol of the element, ether, or universe, or spirit. In modern times, it is associated with the third eye chakra and represents spirit and consciousness.

This shape symbolises the mediation of the infinite and the finite. It is also associated with the planet Earth.

Interestingly, this shape is displayed in some artwork, notably, there is a dodecahedron shaped window behind Christ in 'The Sacrament of the Last Supper', painted by Salvador Dali in 1955. (Martineau, 2016).

The Sacrament of the Last Supper – Salvador Dali

The Icosahedron

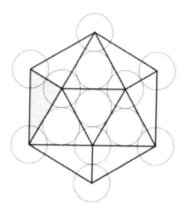

Plato considered the icosahedron to represent the element of water. In modern times, it is associated with the sacral chakra and the emotions.

It spiritually represents a passive trust in the wisdom of the universe and the flow of time. (Usvat, nd).

Using Simple Shapes and Numbers to Create Sacred Geometry

What You Need

To create sacred geometry, you will only need a compass, a protractor, a ruler, a pencil, and paper, and knowledge of the basic shapes previously described in this book. Colour can be added after to enhance the appealing nature of sacred geometry.

But simply drawing geometric shapes is not enough. By applying meanings we find ourselves drawing 'sacred' geometry. The impulse from sacred geometry weaves through heavenly and earthly reality. We can focus on describing creation and consciousness and we can use this to meditate and to attract mystical forces.

"Sacred geometry gives us a beautiful reflection to contemplate as we navigate life's challenges seeking balance and harmony… Shapes, patterns and visual compositions have the capacity to seduce our eyes while captivating our imagination… this entrancement can be so emotionally moving that people naturally associate it with transcendence, the super-natural, or spiritual." (Devaney, 2016).

There are certain sacred geometric patterns that are said to hold specific integral forces within them which I will go on to describe, and drawing and focussing on these is empowering.

The first factor to remember, is that all other geometric shapes can be determined from the circle, which makes the circle all important in creating sacred geometry. It is also the most common shape to occur in nature.

Flower of Life

The Flower of Life Is a hexagonal pattern, starting with one circle with a point in the centre. From there, the centre point of this circle and every circle henceforth is on the circumference of six surrounding circles of the same diameter. In total, there are nineteen complete circles and thirty-six partial circular arcs, enclosed by a large circle.

Flower of Life

The Flower of Life is a significant sacred geometric shape. It represents the fundamental forms of space and time and demonstrates how all things come from one source and are intimately and permanently woven together.

It holds many symbolic significances. In the Qabalah, it is the Tree of Life. It is enlightenment through sacred geometry and the underlying structure of all life. It is thought to be the connection with the universe on a soul level, a portal to other dimensions and worlds, and aligns your energies to a higher vibration.

It is widely used in talismans and magic charms and is considered to channel the magic energy of creation which helps us get closer to creation. It is often used for meditation.

This is an ancient symbol, found in many manuscripts, religious buildings, goblets, textiles, art and jewellery.

The oldest known example of the Flower of Life is found in the Temple of Osiris, at Abydos in Egypt. This is 3000 years old.

Flower of Life found in the Temple of Osiris

Ancient examples can also be found in Phoenician, Assyrian, Indian, Asian, Middle eastern and medieval art.

Further examples of the symbol are in the Forbidden City in China, ancient synagogues in the Galilee and in Mesada, temples in Japan, and in the Harimandir Sahib in India.

Seed of Life

From the Flower of Life, many important scared geometric shape can be derived. One of these is the Seed of Life.

The Seed of Life occurs a stage before the Flower of Life shape emerges. It starts with a circle with a centre point. From there, the centre point of this circle is on the circumference of six surrounding circles of the same diameter, each one's circumference running through the centre point of the one next to it. This is then surrounded by one larger circle.

Seed of Life

This geometric shape is often referred to as the 'rosette' as it resembles a flower and it was traditionally used for decoration in ancient Mesopotamia.

It is thought to represent the Sun, where the petals of the rosette are sunrays.

Many cultures use the rosette to avoid bad luck and the central six petals symbolise blessings. In Eastern Europe the Seed of Life and the Flower of Life were called 'thunder marks' and were carved on buildings to protect them from lightning. (Matthews, 2015).

Some believe that the Seed of Life displays the seven days of Creation. The first day is the creation of the Vesica Pisces (see page 100), the second day is the creation of the Tripod of Life (see page 92). One circle is then added for each subsequent day until all seven circles construct the Seed of Life on the sixth day, with the seventh day being the day of rest.

Fruit of Life

The Fruit of Life is constructed from thirteen circles within the design of the Flower of Life.

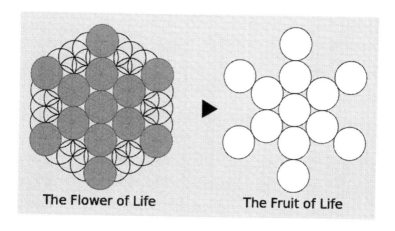

The Flower of Life   The Fruit of Life

The Fruit of Life is a modern symbol and is considered to be the blueprint of the universe. It contains the geometric basis for the construction of Metatron's Cube (see page 95).

Egg of Life

The Egg of Life is constructed from seven circles within the design of the Flower of Life.

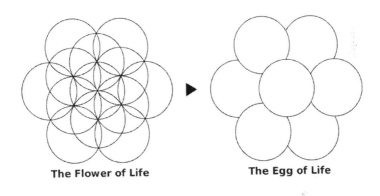

The Flower of Life   The Egg of Life

The Egg of Life is said to symbolise new life, fertility and re-birth. The Egg of Life births the Flower of Life and stands for health and stability. It carries a positive power that encourages ingenuity and inspiration.

Tripod of Life

The Tripod of Life is a component of the Flower of Life, derived from the overlapping of three circles, each perimeter meeting the centre of the other circles.

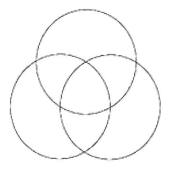

Tripod of Life

This shape is a basic trefoil unit said to represent the energy form of the second day of Creation. It also symbolises Trinity. The centre 'curved' triangle is a Reuleaux triangle, (see page 105), and acts as a lens for powerful energies from higher realms. (Silberberg, 2014).

Tree of Life

Derived from the Flower of Life, the Tree of Life is considered to be a symbol of stability and strength.

Tree of Life

The symbol of the Tree of Life has been adopted by the Jews, Christians and Pagans, and the earliest known examples of this design were drawn by the ancient Egyptians.

It is thought that in the structure of the Tree of Life, ways to return to the divine spirit can be found, while still living in the material world. The sign is also considered to be the illustration of the human mind. (Williams, 2015).

In Celtic culture, the Tree of Life, or 'crann bethadh' represented how the forces of nature combined to create balance and harmony.

It is most widely seen as a concept within the Kabbalah where it was developed into a full model of reality, the tree depicting a map of creation. It has been called the 'cosmology' of the Kabbalah.

Metatron's Cube

Metatron's Cube is a symbol derived from the Fruit of Life. It is composed of thirteen equal circles with lines from the centre of each circle extending out to the centres of the other twelve circles.

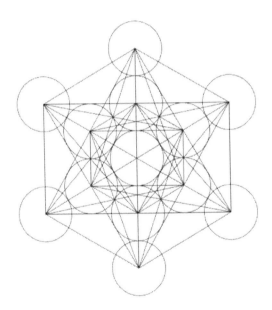

Metatron's Cube

If you create Metatron's Cube in three dimensions, all the Platonic solids can be attained.

Platonic Solids

"Metatron's Cube generated the Platonic solids. These forms created structure throughout the universe" (Melchizedek, 2000).

In Judaism, Metatron is the archangel who guards God's throne. He transmits the daily orders of God to the angels Gabriel and Samuel and is often depicted as holding a cube.

According to myth, Metatron created the cube out of his soul and the cube represents God's energy flowing through Metatron to all parts of creation. It is Metatron's task to ensure the energy flows in the proper balance so that nature will be in harmony.

The name Metatron, comes from the Latin, 'metator', which means, 'one who metes out or marks off a place,' and 'a divider and fixer of boundaries,' and 'a measurer,' and by these translations, is directly related to sacred geometry.

Some say that the thirteen circles of the shape, Metatron's Cube, represent the thirteen centres of energy in our human bodies, or the thirteen keys of creation.

It was often drawn around an object or person to ward off evil spirits and dark entities. (Patinkas, 2014).

Metatron's Cube symbolises the gridwork of our consciousness and the building blocks of the cosmos. It is the matrix in which everything our three dimensional reality is contained. (Tooley, 1997).

Torus

A torus is a surface of revolution generated by revolving a circle in three dimensional space about an axis coplanar with the circle. If the axis of revolution does not touch the circle, the surface has a ring shape, or donut shape.

Torus

The Torus is said to define the workings and self-reflective nature of consciousness, light and energy.

It is the fundamental form of balanced energy flow, either as a descent from spirit or an ascent of matter, channelling through the central tube and then doubling back on itself to return to its original source. During its path, the energy will gain height or depth, before being pulled back in to itself, growing and flourishing, and then diminishing and returning. (Atala, 2019).

In 1984, Russian scientists, Alexie Starobinsky and Yakov Borisovich Zel Dovich, at the Landau Institute, Moscow, devised a cosmological model called the 'Three-Torus Model' which described the shape of the universe as a three dimensional torus, known informally as the 'Doughnut Theory'.

Vesica Piscis

Two overlapping circles create a significant shape called the Vesica Piscis, from which further shapes, such as the triangle, square, and pentagon can be generated.

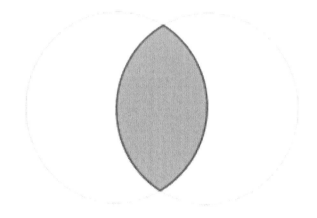

Vesica Piscis

This specific shape is formed by the two overlapping circles having the same radius and intersecting so that the centre of each circle lies on the perimeter of the other.

The term 'vesica piscis' is latin, meaning 'bladder of a fish', which reflects the shape's resemblance to the conjoined dual air bladders found in most fish. (Matthews, 2015).

Two fish swimming in opposite directions, linked by a rope, represents the constellation and zodiac symbol Pisces.

Zodiac Symbol Pisces

Vesica is also a colloquial name for the vagina with reference to its shape, and therefore represents an object of desire for men, and is the feminine symbol of maternity and creation. (Barrallo, 2015).

The Vesica Piscis Symbol is taken to represent the virgin birth in Christianity, and the birth of the universe and everything in it.

In Christian tradition, the Vesica Piscis represents Christ and there are numerous examples of the use of this shape in church architecture. Typically, the windows and doors were often designed as half Vesica Piscis, as displayed in this photo of the Notre Dame in Paris, France.

Notre Dame

The Ichthys is a Christian symbol consisting of a sideways Vesica Pisces resembling a fish, appearing as early as the second century AD. It was used as a secret symbol for Christians during times of persecution by the Romans. It designated meeting places and distinguished Christian brethren from adversaries. (Archer, 2018).

Ichthys

In sacred geometry, curved lines are feminine energy. Straight lines are considered to be masculine energy, so when both are present, creation can occur.

If you refer back to our description of the 'Line' (page 21), for the 'Point' or 'one' to become many, the circle must be reflected, and then a line can be created connecting the two centre circles. Using this method, the principles of all the following numbers can be created. So the feminine and masculine have come together to enable creation.

Line

Therefore the Vesica Piscis is considered to be the 'mother' of geometric shapes, giving birth to the triangle, square and other regular polygons, as well as other sacred geometric shapes, such as the Flower of Life and Seed of Life and their derivatives.

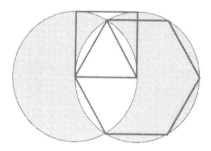

Shapes from the Vesica Pisces

Reuleaux Triangle

The Reuleaux triangle can be generated from the Vesica Piscis, by adding an extra arc, similar to the previous two, to the equilateral triangle created within the overlapping circles.

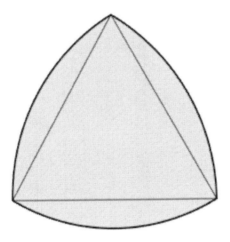

Reuleaux Triangle

The accuracy of the third arc is generated by creating a third circle, of same size to the first two, and over lapping it above and centrally, as in the Tripod of Life, so that its centre meets the top point where the first two circles meet.

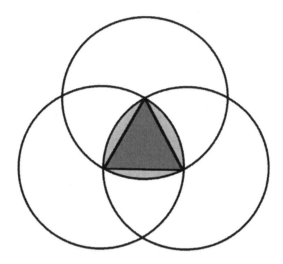

Deriving the Reuleaux Triangle from the Tripod of Life

This shape is named after the German engineer, Franz Reuleaux (1829-1905), and is also referred to as the spherical triangle and the Reuleaux Rotor. It can often be found in furniture design and Gothic architecture. Interestingly, it is also used in drill bits to create square holes. (Barrallo, 2015).

In church architecture, this shape was often used as a window, the three corners being representative of the Trinity.

Reuleaux Triangle as Church Window

In nature, soap bubbles can often be seen to be forming in clusters which generate a three dimensional Reuleaux triangle.

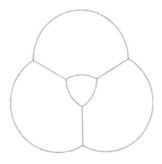

Three dimensional Reuleaux triangle soap cluster formation

Triquetra

The Triquetra is generated from three vesical piscis, and is sometimes depicted with a circle within the three lobes.

Triquetra

This symbol has been used by Celtic Christians and pagans as a sign of anything that is threefold, such as the cycle of life, (life, death, re-birth) and the family, (father, mother, child), and time, (past, present, future).

It also symbolises the female trinity, and is often referred to as the Trinity Knot.

It has been found on runestones in Northern Europe and early Germanic coins and is the symbol of the god, Odin, the Germanic war god associated with wisdom, healing, death, knowledge, sorcery, poetry, battle and the runic alphabet.

In Christian architecture, this symbol can often been seen as the shape of windows and also stained glass within windows, and many examples of the triquetra can be found in Christian manuscripts. It symbolises the Holy Trinity of Father, Son and Holy Spirit. (Forsyth, 2002).

In Irish Celtic culture, the triquetra is referred to as the Irish Love Knot, and is traditionally exchanged between lovers representing eternal love.

Wiccans also use this shape to represent the Triple goddess of as a sign of protection

Triple goddess sign of protection.

Also called the Celtic Trinity Knot or Irish Love Knot.

Tetractys

The Tetractys was devised by Pythagoras (circa 600 BC) and was considered to be so admired, that his students would swear oaths by it.

It is a triangular figure, of four rows which add up to the number ten.

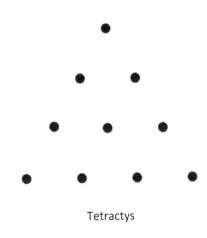

Tetractys

The Tetractys displays the central monad, the mirror image duad, the triangular triad, the four level tetrad, and adds up to the decad. (Parke & Howard, 1993).

The number ten is considered to be completeness, finality and the perfect number, as it is the sum of the numbers one, two, three and four.

Pythagoras believed that reflecting on mathematical truths could shift the psyche closer to the divine perfection of the number gods. (Fincher, 2017).

He said that the power of the number ten, lies in the number four, because, by starting at the number one, and then adding the successive numbers up to four, the perfect number ten is arrived at. (1 + 2 + 3 + 4 = 10). (Hobgood, nd).

Hence, the tetractys is regarded as divine by those who understand it.

The Symbol of Alchemy

The Symbol of Alchemy, also called the Grand Tangent, is represented by a circle within a square, within a triangle, within a larger circle.

Symbol of Alchemy

This symbol also represents the Philosopher's Stone, the ultimate goal of alchemy, first used in the 17th century. The Philosopher's Stone was said to be a substance that alchemists believed would change any base metal into silver and gold. (Beyer, 2019).

Some say, that to correctly draw the Symbol of Alchemy, the small circle and square must be located in the lower half of the larger circle. The lower half of the larger circle represents the material world and the upper half represents the spiritual world. This drawing is referred to as a drawing of the Philosopher's Stone and is considered to be the 'Key to Enlightenment'. (Furstner, 2004).

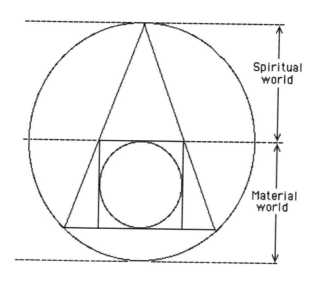

The Philosopher's Stone

Pentagram

The pentagram is a five pointed star, constructed from a pentagon.

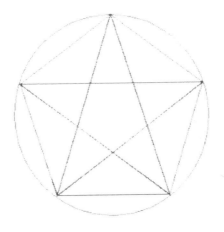

Pentagram

A Golden pentagram, is one whose five equal triangular extremities are Golden triangles.

The pentagram is often displayed within a circle, and has had many historic religious and spiritual meanings in various cultures.

Around 3500 BC, Pentagrams were used in Mesopotamian writings. They also appeared in ancient Egyptian, Greek and Roman art.

The ancient Babylonians used the pentagram to symbolise a number of gods.

In his book, Pentamychos, Pherecydes of Syros (500 AD), said the pentagram was a mystical symbol of the cosmos. He said that the recesses of the star represented the chambers in which primordial chaos was sealed so that an ordered cosmos could appear. (Wright, 2017).

In 1100 AD, the nun, Hildegard of Bingen said that the pentagram represented humans, as we have five senses, sight, smell, hearing, taste and touch, and we have five extremities, two arms, two legs and a head. She claimed that as humans are made in Gods image, the pentagram therefore also represents God.

In the Middle Ages, the five points of the pentagram came to symbolise the five knightly virtues. In the poem, Sir Gawain and the Green Knight, the points of the pentagram represent chastity, chivalry, courtesy, generosity, and piety. (Gardner, 2003).

It was also often carved above doors and windows to protect the occupants and ward off devils and witches.

Many churches exhibit the pentagram within their architecture, the five points of the star representing the five Joys Mary had of Christ; the Annunciation, the Nativity, the Resurrection, the Ascension, and the Assumption.

Pentacle

In popular culture today, the pentagram, often called the pentacle, is usually displayed in a circle and is often thought of as a pagan or wicca symbol, or a symbol of witchcraft. The five points represent the elements, water, fire, earth, air and spirit, with further symbols for each element, and the circle represents the universe and contains and connects the elements. (Wright 2017).

Wiccan Pentagram

There is also a popular belief that a downward pointed pentagram is the symbol of Satan and devil worship, though this is disputed.

Hexagram (Star of David / Solomon's Seal)

The hexagram is a six pointed star, constructed from two equilateral triangles derived from the hexagon, often displayed in a circle.

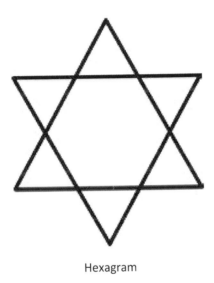

Hexagram

In South Indian Hindu temples, the hexagram is a mandala, symbolising a perfect meditative state achieved between Man and God. It is called the Nara-Narayana, and it is said to point to heaven and earth, drawing them together. Nara and Narayana were two inseparable sages, twins, who defeated a demon called Sahasrakavacha for the sake of mankind. (Nair, 2013).

The upward triangle represents Shiva, (fire and masculinity). The downward triangle represents Shakti, (the sacred embodiment of femininity). The union of the two represents creation. The two locked triangles are known as Shanmukha, or six-faced, which represents the six faces of Shiva and Shakti's progeny, Kartikeya.

Star of David

The Hexagram is also the Star of David. It is often referred to as the Shield of David or the Magen David, and it is named after King David of Israel. Today, it is the symbol of the Jewish religion and the State of Israel. It first became associated with the Jewish community in Prague in 1300 AD.

The Star of David has seven compartments. Six peaks and the centre. The peaks are said to contain kindness, severity, harmony, perseverance, splendour, and royalty. The centre contains Foundation, to which the others are rooted in and arise from. (Silberberg, 2008).

Solomon's Seal

King Solomon was the son of David. Solomon's Seal, also known as the Ring of Solomon, and Seal of Solomon, was depicted as a magic signet ring, which gave Solomon the power to command demons and speak with animals. It was said to have been engraved by God and given to the King from heaven. (Mingren, 2016).

Solomon's Seal

There are several versions of what is thought to be Solomon's Seal. Some site a difference between the Star of David and Solomon's Seal, in that the Star of David has only intersecting triangles, whereas the Seal of Solomon has interlaced triangles:

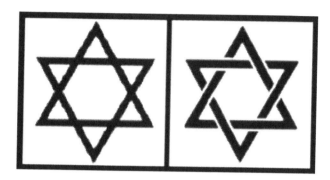

Venus Cycle

The pattern of Venus orbiting the sun thirteen times traces out a curve called the 'Pentagram of Venus', so called because the five lobes ascribe where Venus makes its closest approach to Earth. At the point of each closest approach there are five synods where Venus appears to move backwards in retrograde motion, compared to its usual motion across the sky. (Baez, 2014).

Venus Cycle

"During this eight year period Venus draws an elegant pentagonal rose pattern against the backdrop of the sky, and on completion after the eight solar / thirteen Venus years she is back to almost the same starting point." (Glyn-Jones, 2009).

The ancient Egyptians used the five pointed star, or pentacle, to represent this cycle.

Eight Pointed Star

It takes eight Earth years for Venus to orbit the sun thirteen times, or for this curve to be traced. In ancient Sumer, circa 4000 BC, this cycle was recognised and they represented it with an eight pointed star, which they also associated with the goddess Inanna, the Sumerian mother goddess of love, beauty, sex, desire, fertility, procreation, war and justice.

The Babylonians used an eight pointed starburst symbol to represent the goddess Ishtar, goddess of love, sexuality, fertility and war, sharing many of the same aspects as the Sumerian goddess Inanna. (Beyer, 2019).

Eight Pointed Star

It is also common for the eight sided star to be featured in Christian church ceilings

This eight year cycle can also be represented by an octagon, where each point is the position of Venus in her solar orbit on the same day of each of the eight different years.

Rose

The rose is derived from the Pentagram of Venus, and was called such because of its five petalled shape.

Rose

This shape was used in ancient Rome to represent the goddess Venus, goddess of love, beauty, desire, sex, fertility, prosperity and victory and was the symbol of womanhood and natural beauty.

In 3000 BC, the Egyptians associated this symbol with the sky god Horus, the half hawk, half man god of power and wisdom. To the Greeks, Horus was the god of silence, and hence this symbol became associated with secrecy.

In Christianity, the rose represented the Virgin Mary, in Islam it is a symbol of the human soul, and in Buddhism and Hinduism it is believed to be an expression of joy.

The 'Cinquefoil' (which means five leaves in French), is a simplified version of the rose, and was known as the 'Rose of Venus' by the Romans.

Cinquefoil

This symbol can often be found in Christian church architecture, above Gothic arches or as decorative windows.

Mandalas

In Hindu and Buddhist symbolism, a traditional mandala is a circular figure representing the universe. They are geometric designs made through uniform and repeated divisions of the circle. They are thought to reveal the inner workings of nature and the inherent order of the universe. They link the human consciousness to the infinite by acting as a bridge between the higher and lower realms.

Today, many cultures use mandalas to represent the cosmos metaphysically and symbolically to focus attention, as a spiritual guidance tool, to establish a sacred space and as an aid to meditation and relaxation.

In the early 20th century, psychologist Carl Jung recognised that the urge to make mandalas occurred during moments of intense personal growth. He said that the need to draw them indicated a re-balancing was taking place, and that by drawing mandalas, one could help stabilise, integrate and re-order inner life.

Mandala

"The mandala is an archetypical image whose occurrence is attested throughout the ages... The circular image represents the wholeness, or, to put in mythic terms, the divinity incarnate in man." (Carl Jung, 1963).

The traditional Hindu and Buddhist mandalas are square, with four gates in a T-shape, containing a circle with a centre point, and it can represent the entire universe.

In Buddhism, mandalas can be found on temple floors around the world. Specific mandalas are traditionally created by Buddhist monks for use in ceremonies, using fourteen colours, and they relate to the symbol of a palace and a deity. They say that regarding a mandala, clears away disease and negative energies that impede spiritual growth. (Tana, 2009).

Traditional Mandala

The ancient Egyptians created mandalas with the god Horus at the centre, and his four sons at each corner.

In the Middle Ages, Christian mandalas were popular for prayer, and often depicted Christ in the centre, with the four evangelists at the cardinal points.

Today, mandala like mosaics can be seen in Gothic church architecture on floors and in stained glass windows called rose windows, or Catherine windows.

Church Rose Window

Mandalas have recently become popular to draw, and appear as graphic forms in adult colouring books as an aid to relaxation.

Yantras

A Yantra is a type of mandala that visually represents the harmonic tones of mantras. The word itself comes from the Sanskrit words 'yam', which means to support the essence of an object, and 'tra', or 'trana', which means freedom from bondage. Together, 'Yantra', means liberation from birth and re-birth. (Das, 2019).

They were mystical diagrams used in the tantric traditions of Indian religions for the worship of specific deities and as an aid to meditation and can be up to ten thousand years old.

They traditionally have several geometric shapes, which each hold specific meanings, radiating concentrically from the centre, including points (unity), circles (perfection and blissful void), triangles (feminine energy), hexagons (creation), squares (universal evolution), and lotus petals (purity and variety). The outside often includes a square representing the four cardinal directions, with doors to each. They are generally smaller than other mandalas and use a more limited colour palate.

Shiva Yantra

Meditating on yantra designs is intended to allow their essence to penetrate our minds and bring us closer to the universal consciousness.

Sri Yantra

The Sri Yantra, or 'Yantra of Creation', or 'Navayoni Chakra', or 'Queen of Yantras', is the most revered of all the Hindu yantras. It is believed to be the image of the OM mantra, which is a sacred utterance in Sanskrit that has spiritual powers and is considered to be the primordial sound of creation.

When represented in three dimensions, it is called the 'Maha Meru' as it represents Mount Meru, the cosmic mountain at the centre of the universe. (Das, 2019).

The Sri Yantra is mathematically precise and consists of nine interlocking triangles that surround a central point known as a bindu. These triangles represent the cosmos and the human body. The size and shape of these triangles vary and intersect to form forty three smaller triangles, organised in five concentric levels. Together, they symbolise the totality of the cosmos and express 'Advaita', or non-duality. In the middle, the Bindu (or power point), represents the cosmic centre.

The triangles are surrounded by two concentric circles of eight and sixteen lotus petals which represent the lotus of creation and reproductive vital force. This entire symbol is framed by the broken lines of an earth square which represents a temple with four doors open on to the regions of the universe.

Sri Yantra

The Sri Yantra represents the masculine and feminine divine. The four upward pointing isosceles triangles represent the goddess's masculine embodiment, Shiva, while the five downward pointing triangles symbolize the female embodiment, Shakti.

"To immerse oneself in such a geometric diagram is to enter into a kind of philosophic contemplation." (Lawlor, 1982).

Sri Yantra

When used for meditation, the Sri Yantra is the tool for material manifestation and for obtaining and fulfilling all worldly desires by increasing the focus and clarity of the mind. (Joshi, 2015).

Conclusion

The aim of this book has been to provide a basic understanding of the history, creation and meanings of sacred geometry, and to open an insight into the beliefs placed upon them.

It is important to remember that this is a brief general overview. Sacred geometry is an enormous topic, with many differing schools of thought over the interpretations, representations and symbolisms of each geometric shape. There are several further subjects of sacred geometric importance, including the Archimedean Solids and the Harmony and Music of the Spheres, and more, which if the subject is to be taken seriously, should be researched.

If this book has served to increase your interest in this subject, then it is worthwhile reading further. There are full volumes written about each individual topic within this book with a vast amount of knowledge to digest. Sacred geometry is a subject on which more and more is being learnt. For example, we have talked briefly about three dimensional shapes, but imagine the use of four dimensional shapes in sacred geometry. Some say that time is the fourth dimension. Others say that there are many more as yet undetected dimensions within our universe. And if sacred geometry is the blueprint of our universe, then we have only just scratched the surface of the subject.

The simplified basic outline of sacred geometry within this book will also serve to enable you to begin to create your own sacred geometry, if so desired. Assuming you have an inner spiritual motivation, you can choose shapes with meanings that resonate with your thoughts, and then use these to relax, focus and meditate.

Remember, it is the choice of symbolism and the application of thought and meaning while creating your shape, that make your chosen geometric creation sacred.

End

Glossary of Terms

	Page
Alchemy	113
Cinquefoil	127
Cube	77
Decad	52
Decagon	53
Divine Proportion	60
Dodecahedron	80
Duad	19
Egg of Life	91
Ennead	48
Equilateral Triangle	25
Fibonacci Numbers	57
Fibonacci Spiral	63
Flower of Life	85
Fruit of Life	90
Golden Mean	60
Golden Number	60
Golden Pentagram	115
Golden Ratio	60
Golden Rectangle	61
Golden Section	60
Golden Spiral	63
Golden Triangle	24
Grand Tangent	113
Heptad	40

Heptagon	42
Hexad	36
Hexagram	119
Hexagon	38
Hexahedron	77
Irrational Numbers	55
Icosahedron	82
Isosceles Triangle	24
Maha Meru	135
Mandalas	128
Metatron's Cube	95
Monad	15
Navayoni Chakra	135
Nonagon	50
Octagon	46
Octahedron	79
Ogdaad	44
Pentacle	117
Pentad	33
Pentagon	34
Pentagram	115
Pentagram of Venus	123
Philosopher's Stone	113
Platonic Solids	75
Point	17
Pyramid	73
Queen of Yantras	135
Reuleaux Triangle	105

Rose	126
Rose of Venus	127
Seed of Life	88
Septagon	42
Solomon's Seal	121
Sphere	72
Square	28
Sri Yantra	135
Star of David	120
Star Tetrahedron	77
Sublime Triangle	24
Symbol of Alchemy	113
Tetractys	111
Tetrad	27
Tetrahedron	76
Triad	23
Tree of Life	93
Torus	98
Tripod of Life	92
Triquetra	108
Venus Cycle	123
Vesica Piscis	100
Yantras	133
Yantra of Creation	135

References

Archer, D. (2018) Sacred Symbolism of Vesica Piscis. www.creationcenter.org

Ashley, (2014) The Awakened State. www.theawakenedstate.net

Atala, (2019) The Torus. www.crystal-life.com

Baez, J. (2014) The Pentagram of Venus. www.johncarlosbaez.wordpress.com

Barrallo, J. (2015) An Introduction to the Vesica Piscis, the Reuleaux Triangle and Related Geometric Constructions in Modern Architecture. www.link.springer.com

Beyer, C. (2019) Religion and Spirituality. www.thoughtco.com

Champoux, P. & Buehler, W. S. (1999) Gaia Matrix: Arkhom & the Geometries of Destiny in the North American Landscape. Franklin Media.

Das, S. (2019) What are Yantras? www.thoughtco.com

Devaney, J. (2016) Is Sacred Geometry a Key for Enlightenment. www.upliftconnect.com

Dimurlo, L. (2013) Square Meaning. www.sunsigns.org

Emerson, D. (1996) Mars /Earth Enigma: A Sacred Message to Mankind. United States, Galde Press Inc.

Fincher, S. F. (2017) Creating Mandalas with Sacred Geometry. Shambhala Publications Inc.

Forsyth, S. (2002) Trinity Knot Meanings. www.celtic-weddingrings.com

Furster, C. (2004) The Secret of the Stone. www.ozemail.com.au

Garant, C. G. (2011) Design Metaphysics: The Decagon. www.designconsciousness.blogspot.com

Garant, C. G. (2012) Design Metaphysics: The Platonic Solids. www.designconsciousness.blogspot.com

Gardner, G. (2003) A Sacred Geometry Primer. www.geomancygroup.org

Glyn-Jones, W. (2009) The Sacred Geometry of Sacred Time. www.grahamhancock.com

Godwin, J. (2004) Tetractys. www.allaboutheaven.org

Hobgood, K (nd), Pythagoras and the Mystery of Numbers. www.Jwilson.coe.uga.edu

Holloway, A. (2013) The Golden Ratio – A Sacred Number that Links the Past to the Present. www.ancient-origins.net

Hunt, M. (2007) The Early Christian Symbols of the Octagon and the Fish. www.agapebiblestudy.com

Jaffe, E. (2001) Dictionary of Symbolism. www.umich.edu

Joshi, R. (2015) The Pineal Gland & Symbol of Manifestation – The Sri Yantra. www.powerthoughtsmeditationclub.com

Jung, C. (1963) Memories Dreams and Reflections. Fontana Press, New Ed (1995)

Kahn, L. (2013) The Fibonacci 60 Digit Repeat Cycle. www.lucienkhan.blogspot.com

Kumar, A. (2017) What is the Significance of Number 9 in Hinduism. www.quora.com

Krystleyez, (2018) The Circle / Sphere. www.krystleyez.com

Lawlor, R. (1982) Sacred Geometry: Philosophy and Practice (Art and Imagination). London, Thames & Hudson Ltd

Leiben, J. O. (2018) Sacred Geometry for Artists, Dreamers, and Philosophers: Secrets of Harmonic Creation. Inner Traditions Publishers.

Love, P. (2019) Spiritual Meaning of Numbers. www.universeofsymbolism.com

Lundy, M. (2008) Sacred Geometry. New York, Walker Publishing Company.

Lundy, M. & Sutton, D. et al. (2010) Quadrivium: The Four Classic Liberal Arts of Number, Geometry, Music and Cosmology. Glastonbury, Wooden Books.

Malkowski, E.F. (2007) The Spiritual Technology of Ancient Egypt: Sacred Science and the Mystery of Consciousness. Inner Traditions

Martineau, J. (2016) Dodecahedron. www.dodecahedron.us

Matthews, C. L. (2015) Sacred Geometry: The Seed of Life, Vesica Piscis and the Merkaba

Meisner, G. (2012) The Human Face and the Golden Ratio. www.goldennumber.net

Melchizedek, D. (2000) The Ancient Secret of The Flower of Life, Volume 2. Flagstaff, Light Technology Publishing.

Mingren, W (2016) The Significance of the Sacred Seal of Solomon and its Symbols. www.ancient-origins.net

Nair, B. (2013) The Legend of Krishna: Nara & Narayana. www.vipsana-vidushika.com

Oldale, R. (2017) Hexagon. www.mastermindcontent.co.uk

Parke, G. A. R. & Howard, C. M. (1993) Space Structures 4, Volume 2. London, Thomas Telford Services Ltd.

Patinkas, (2014) The Merkaba, Platonic Solids & Sacred Geometry. www.patinkas.co.uk

Pike, A. (2016) Morals and Dogma of the Ancient and Accepted Scottish Rite of Freemasonry. Washington, Devoted Publishing

Rawles, B. (2012) Sacred Geometry Introductory Tutorial. www.geometrycode.com

Rea, S. (2007) What's So Sacred About the Number 108? www.yogajournal.com

Reynolds, M. (2010) The Octagon in Leonardo's Drawings. www.markreynolds.com

Rogers, S. (2010) Symbiation – Part Seven. www.yogaflavouredlife.com

Scott, H. (2019) Why 7-Sided Design? – Sacred Geometry. www.visioningspaces.org

Silva, F (nd) The Divine Blueprint, Temples, Power Places and the Global Plan to Shape the Human Soul.

Silberberg, B. (2014) Mesa Creative Arts. www.mesacreativearts.com

Silberberg, N. (2008) Star of David: The Mystical Significance. www.chabad.org

Simmons, J. R. (nd) Fibonacci Numbers and Nature. www.jwilson.coe.uga.edu

Skinner, S. (2006) Sacred Geometry Deciphering the Code. New York, Sterling Publishing Co.

Solà-Soler, J. (2012) Phi in the Great Pyramid. www.sacred-geometry.es

Stewart, I. (2005) Number Symbolism. www.britannica.com

Tana, M. (2009) Mandalland. www.mandalland.blogspot.com

Tooley, A. (1997) Sacred Geometry. www.energyandvibration.com

Usvat, L. (nd) Sacred Geometry and the Platonic Solids. www.mathematicsmagazine.com

Venefica, A (2013) Spiral Meaning. www.whats-your-sign.com

Welman, M. (2016) Pi and Spirituality. www.kabbalahmadeeasy.com

Williams, H. (2015) Sacred Geometry: Tree of Life. www.medium.com

Wright, M. S. (2017) Pentagram and Pentacle Defined for Beginner Wiccans. www.exemplore.com

Yogev, N. (2018) The Meaning of Number 6. www.purecosmetics.info

Connect with the author

www.facebook.com/DebbieBrewerPoetry

www.instagram.com/poetrytreasures

www.twitter.com/poetrytreasure

www.debbiebrewerauthor.com

Made in the
USA
Lexington, KY